THE TECHNIQUE OF RAISED GILDING

BY
JERRY TRESSER

MICHELLE JORDAN PUBLICATIONS

Something attempted, something done, has earned a nights repose.
LONGFELLOW

Acknowledgments

Thank you friends of the Society of Scribes and many other calligraphic societies throughout the USA for saying "You should write a book on the subject." For the wonderful help that I received from the scientific community, I am indebted to Dr. Martin Mizel, Dr. Steven Anolik, Dr. David Bernstein (Toxicology Dept. Brookhaven Labs), Dr. Joseph Pierce (Neurobiology Dept. Stonybrook University). To Matthew Murray of Tranquility Base Inc., for helping me put the manuscript together, and of course the love of my life my wonderful wife Leah.

Copyright© 1992 Jerry Tresser

All rights reserved. No part of this book may be reproduced or transmitted in any form or by any means, graphic, electronic, or mechanical including photocopying, recording, taping or by any information, storage and retrieval system, without written permission from the publisher.

Michelle Jordan Publications
4 Stacy Court
Port Jefferson, New York. 11777
ISBN # 0-9633173-0-X
Typeset by
Karma Dog Editions
P.O. Box 42 Ridge N.Y. 11961
Printed in the United States of America

This book is dedicated to
the loving memory of my brother
Ronny

Foreword

In the kingdom of gilding, all roads lead to Cennino Cennini.

This book is a practical but scientific reevaluation of Cennini's method for raised gilding. Raised gilding refers to a type of gilding best suited for book illumination and the illumination of single works of art on paper or vellum. It does not include architectural or furniture gilding, gilding on glass, or mural, fresco and panel gilding. Considered by many to be the highest form of the craft, this technique is often tried by American lettering artists who wish to embellish their own work.

The conundrum of 20th century gilding has been the gap between historical examples of manuscript illumination and our own torturous attempts to emulate those models. We have ample opportunity to study illuminated works in our museums and libraries, and to note the best qualities of the craft: the high burnish of the gold, the marble-like smoothness of the gesso, and the longevity of the bright metallic effect. While inspired and guided by historical models, we are at a loss to reproduce their effect with the apparent ease and frequency demonstrated by medieval craftsmen.

Many modern gilders have, in good faith, tried to reproduce the aesthetic effect of medieval manuscript gilding by applying a traditional interpretation of Cennini's formula. The results have been notoriously inconsistent in the short term, and some examples of apparently successful gilding have gradually succumbed to orange peel textures, cloudy burnishes, and cracked gessoes.

Undaunted by such setbacks, today's resourceful calligraphers employ an amazingly wide variety of ingenious techniques that adequately get the job done. The fact remains that many American calligraphers have come to regard raised gilding as witchcraft, not artistic craft. We have come to appreciate plaster-based gessoes as fickle media. We are taught that raised gilding is a quirky procedure with a mind of its own, and we are eventually put off by its impractical mumbo jumbo. (Modern gilders should not be required to sequester themselves in steamy bathrooms in order to lay down gold. After all, medieval scriptoria did not provide saunas for their illuminators.)

The net effect of this technical frustration is a diminution of artistic expression. A calligrapher cannot cut loose and really begin to paint with raised gilding if he or she is hobbled by an unreliable technique. No calligrapher looks forward to the possible ruination of an important work for the sake of a single gold initial. Furthermore, no responsible calligrapher should utilize a technique that might prove to be unstable or non-permanent over the long term.

American calligraphers tend to be inventive and individualistic in their interpretation of the craft of calligraphy. They are free to express their message without the burden of paying homage to a national tradition of illumination calligraphy . They are strongly influenced by the practical requirements of advertising art, private press books, display lettering, magazine graphics and the like. Their creative inclinations require artistic media that are reliable, dependable and consistent, and which readily subordinate themselves to the desired artistic effect.

This practical attitude towards the lettering arts and decoration is an historically authentic approach to the craft of illuminated calligraphy. Craft implies utility, and gilding is expected to serve a useful purpose: the decorative qualities of letters should be respected and enhanced by the metal, or some aspect of the textural content should be illumined by the gold. However, a satisfying balance between metal and letters can only be achieved through control of technique; and technical proficiency is based on a thorough knowledge of why and how a medium handles as it does. This knowledge is requisite for any serious craftsman.

It is impractical or impossible for each of us to chemically dissect the gessoes of medieval manuscripts and thus obtain a definitive recipe for their manufacture. But a high tech approach is not really necessary for our success because the formula for raised gilding has been in print for hundreds of years--if only we knew what all the words really meant! The author of this book, believing in the credibility of Cennini's formula, went back to the basics and conducted a linguistic analysis of Cennini's text. The dissection of language has yielded up the original, intended procedure for raised gilding. The methodology has been confirmed by scientific instrumentation and experiment.

The book is an essential point of departure for those calligrapher-illuminators who wish to gain more control over their craft through knowledge of its mechanics and achieve greater artistic self-expression in their work.

Sally Secrist
Milford, Ohio

A 12" letter interfaced 12 times. The gesso had been thined considerably for easy use.

Preface

The philosopher Albert North Whitehead argued that "The artist doesn't know what he knows in general, he only knows what he knows specifically. What he knows in general...becomes apparent later on by what he has had to put down."[1] Jerry Tresser is very specific, and he has two specific reasons for doing so: first, he offers a more efficient approach to a particular technique; second, he corrects some common misapplications of this technique.

Not to imply that there is only one correct Medieval gilding technique: many of the gilding practices of the Middle Ages were already known to the Romans - they are described by Pliny the Elder (23 - 79 CE), one of the best known authors of the Roman Empire.[2] Nevertheless, the technique discussed here was originally meant for the vellum pages of a book, and since Book Illumination on vellum developed only in the Middle Ages, it is to this period that Tresser returns.

When a unified European culture began to emerge after the fall of the Roman Empire new techniques of gilding developed for manuscript illumination. By the eight century the manuscripts of Northern France, England and Germany showed an innovative use of garlic juice for gilding, but other arts like painting, jewelry, mosaic or metalwork continued to depend on Roman techniques. It was probably a German metalsmith, Theophilus Presbyter, who in the twelfth century wrote one of the most thorough documents we have on Medieval gilding. For gilding in books, theophilus followed the common practice of *fondo d'oro* (gold background) gilding: a cushion of red earth was built up with gelatin or glair, then covered with gold, in a manner still reminiscent of Pliny.[3]

The late twelfth century ushered in enormous changes. Europe moved from debtor to creditor nation, from a rural to a city based economy, from Romanesque style to Gothic. By the early thirteenth century tastes in manuscripts and paintings shifted from an emphasis on broad, unmodulated areas of color to more refined contrast of details. Where previously a solid mass of gold would have filled the background of a Romanesque page or panel, the Gothic craftsperson (male or female), would paint a series of small illuminated letters or patterns to catch the eye. And since these new manuscripts were now intended for private use rather than display, as previously, the vellum of the pages was shaved thin for a more flexible, easier-to-turn, page. Thereafter, many recipes for gilding on vellum required lead and sugar (or honey), to insure that the gilding would not crack as the pages were turned. The techniques for gilding walls and painted panels changed little from those described by Theophilus and Pliny, though there is some evidence of experimentation, especially in twelfth and thirteenth century Sicily.

This two-fold approach according to the medium explains why the Italian artist Cennino Cennini offers two different sets of recipes in his Libro dell'Arte of 1399 - one for solid surfaces, another for books.[4] Cennini, a late follower of Giotto, was more of a fresco and panel painter than a book-artist, and as I have suggested elsewhere,[5] his recipes for gilding on books were probably meant to fulfill an occasional request. For instance, he uses "gesso sottile," a by-product of panel preparation; and he only calls for white lead and sugar in his recipe for gilding in manuscripts.

In Anglo-Saxon countries a movement to revive Medieval craftsmanship began in 1834, when the Houses of Parliament at Westminster burned down. Over the next decades the artists and critics of England debated which styles would be appropriate for rebuilding and redecorating this symbol of the British Nation. The Gothic style seemed most appropriate, since the British believed themselves to be a Germanic race. A large-scale effort to translate and clarify Medieval technical manuals was undertaken, notably by Sir Charles Eastlake (President of the Royal Academy of Art), and Mary Philadelphia Merrifield. Merrifield translated Cennini into English and published numerous other similar works.[6] An incredible upsurge of interest in Medieval techniques followed, including of course manuscript illumination and gilding. This was more of a revival than a recovery, since the old traditions still remained in the luxury trades. The main difference was, that being "Medieval" was now fashionable posture for the upper and middle classes.

Cennini's recipe for gilding in manuscripts owes some of its present glamour to William Morris, a wealthy manufacturer and designer as well as a major poet of the late nineteenth century. Morris had a life-long fascination with the Middle Ages, but later in life he transferred his beliefs from the Victorian upper-class dream of a reactionary feudal order in which men were knights, serfs knew their place, and all but the English were an inferior race, to a Socialist vision of the Middle Ages that promised paradise on Earth, not simply in Heaven. This accounts for his preference for late Medieval Italian styles (including Cennini), over Northern Gothic; for a style in transition over a style frozen in time; for individual improvisation over blind antiquarianism.[7]

Morris' artistry deeply marked the Arts and Crafts Movement of the late nineteenth and early twentieth century - more so than his beliefs. The names of Edward Johnston, Graily Hewitt, W. R. Lethaby, are familiar to modern-day illuminators. Less familiar, unfortunately, are names like Phoebe Traquair, Jessie Bayes and Florence Kingsford, all women, all preeminent gilders in their day, all excluded from such influential networks as the Art Workers' Guild.[8]

The Morris style dominated gilding and writing throughout World War One, partly because the anti-German attitude of the times required a move away from Gothic styles, partly because the large demand for memorial books to commemorate the war dead required gilding on vellum pages, and mostly because English craftspeople slipped into anachronism and nostalgia. Meanwhile in Germany, the Arts and Crafts movement inspired a renewal of industrial design that culminated in the Bauhaus. Today the last survivors of the English movement are less likely to follow the Socialist Morris than the conservatives John Ruskin and Matthew Arnold, with inflated calls for "preserving the traditions of the past." The irony is that it is a past manufactured out of whole cloth; the tragedy is, that those who hide behind imaginary "secrets of the medieval scribe" mostly do so to protect themselves from criticism and competition. This is not Medievalism as Morris would have understood it: "What business have we with art at all, if we cannot share it?"[9]

What Tresser shares with us revives the only past worth living, the kind that provides a bridge to the future. Humanity does not begin any new work, but consciously brings about the completion of the old.

P.T. Werner
N.Y., N.Y.

Table of Contents

Foreword v

Preface ix

Introduction 15

Chapter One: Preparing the Gesso 23

Chapter Two: Applying the Gesso 34

Chapter Three: Applying the Gold 39

    Special Preparations 46

Conclusion 52

Glossary 54

Works Cited 58

Footnotes to Preface 59

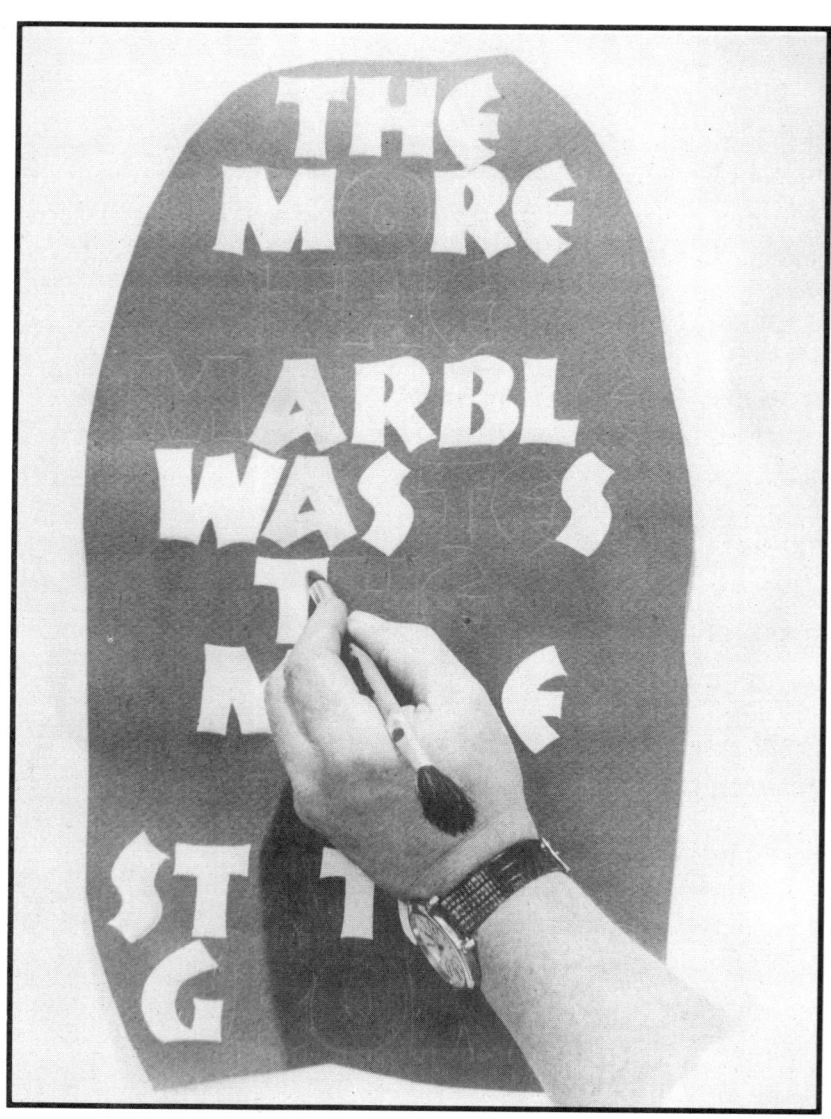

When properly made the gesso can be built up to any desired height or size, providing that you interface each layer and allow it to dry before adding on the next layer. Thin layers of gesso were interfaced four times on each letter over a period of 7 days

Introduction

St. Jerome inveighed against the worldliness and extravagance of the gold and purple codices: "skins are dyed with the color purple, gold melts into letters, the books are clothed with gems - and Christ is left standing naked outside the door" (Quoted from Mat. and Tech., 199).

The early Christian love of ornate illuminated manuscripts extended through the Middle Ages, and even today a single page from a medieval manuscript easily fetches in excess of fifty thousand dollars. The illuminator's craft was once regarded as equal to the painter's and though few people today practice it professionally, there is perhaps a growing interest in this craft, as people turn increasingly away from commercial products and toward products which bear the mark of a single unique hand.

Any work that purports to provide information on how to do something is valuable only to the extent that the information is understandable and workable. This is the first and only workable book devoted to the techniques of raised gilding. It is written for use by beginners or experts. Since gilding comes to us from the fourteenth century, this is not the first work on the subject; in fact, several have been written in the latter half of this century alone. Yet like a story often repeated, at ten removes from the teller it is no longer the same story. The same may be said about the gilding techniques of the medieval masters: at six hundred years removed, their methods, as they appear in currently practiced versions, are no longer workable, except on a trial and error basis.

Until now. This book rejects the current techniques, and returns to the source for its information, interprets this information in a new and more careful manner, and combines the information with some basic advances in chemistry since that medieval time. The result is a book which provides a gilding method that is reliable and workable each time it is used, whether the user is a first time gilder or a practiced expert.

As the title suggests, this book will explain how to perform raised gilding. You will find that the structure has been determined by the order of operations necessary to gild, so that you as a reader are quite literally led through the process step by step. This structure will enable you to use the book as guide and companion while you work. The book begins with this section, which provides both an explanation of the scope of techniques I will discuss, as well as a historical framework for those techniques.

In the interest of serving you, the how-to user best, each section begins with a list of materials you will need to perform the operations in that section. These lists function like ingredients lists in recipes for food, and like them, it is best to gather all your materials before you begin the processes. Additionally, the sections are ordered according to the order of steps you would need to follow to perform raised gilding from the ground up. So, you will find chapter one describes how to prepare the gesso base you will need to apply to the surface on which you're gilding; chapter two describes this application process; chapter three discusses how to apply gold to this gesso base you have now put down, and also describes additional techniques related to the project of raised gilding: and finally, there is a glossary of tools, materials, and chemicals along with a brief description of the use of each item. This last section is designed as a reference to the reader who finds himself in unfamiliar territory at any point in his reading.

Background:
Distinguishing Raised Gilding From Flat Gilding

Gold illumination was originally performed using gold ink. The technique, called chrysography, allowed the illuminator to simply write directly onto his surface. This ink was made of gold powder mixed with some kind of sticky substance, such as glair or gum arabic. The ink was very expensive, both to make and to use: in order to obtain the gold powder in the ink the illuminator made shavings of gold coins, and then proceeded to grind these shavings to a powder. But the process was made more difficult because the gold shavings tended to stick to themselves due to the natural softness of gold itself. Even once he had made a powdered gold and mixed it with his mordant, or adhesive material, he found that a great deal of gold was required to draw even a modest-sized letter or leaf decoration.

At some time prior to the twelfth century, when records began to be kept, illuminators discovered that gold leaf would adhere to a sticky surface, and this surface could later be burnished, when dry, to a brilliant golden shine. The visual effect they achieved with gold leaf was the same as that using gold powder, yet the leaf was far easier to manufacture, and far less costly because far less of it was required to cover a given surface area. This ancient method of flat gilding has remained in use on up to today, and is generally used to cover large surfaces such as grounds, on which letters or designs of various colors are painted.

Raised gilding began to be used after flat gilding when illuminators discovered that they could mix their glue with a chalk or powder to give it body; that they could apply this pasty material to their flat surface and build up those areas where they applied it; and that when they applied gold leaf on top of those areas and then burnished them, it appeared that their letter or design was a solid piece of gold that had somehow adhered to the surface. The effect of this raising from the flat surface was not only dramatic but also created a quite tactile richness upon an otherwise smooth surface. This raised effect was traditionally used to cover small areas, such as letters, smaller figures, leaf or scroll work, and halos. And today, it is still used as an adornment on colored grounds, rather than as a ground itself as is the case with flat gilding.

An Historical Perspective of Raised Gilding

This raised form of gilding began to be practiced in the fourteenth century. It comprised a resplendent but brief chapter in medieval art, and since it was generally reserved for the lettering and adorning of hand-written manuscripts, it passed almost entirely from use by the end of the fifteenth century, with the coming of the printing press. Raised gilding techniques remained all but extinct until the nineteenth century when the manuscripts of certain medieval Italian masters were discovered and translated into English. These translations allowed William Morris, among others, to re-discover the techniques of gilding. Morris was at the head of a movement among English artists and writers which disavowed the industrialism that clutched England at the time, and which favored instead a harkening back to medieval artistic subjects and practices.

There are two works, Il Libro dell'Arte by Cennino Cennini, and De Arte Illuminandi whose author is unknown, which describe all known painting methods in Italy at the end of the fourteenth century, (De Arte, VIII). Both of these books are practical guides for students of painting, and it is from translations of them that Morris and others acquired the techniques of the medieval arts of gilding, calligraphy and so on which were lost after 1500.

Now, these two works were not the only ones written at the time, but they are the only ones which were found to be clearly enough written to be of value to students of these arts five hundred years later. Of the two of them, Cennini's is the clearest, and is the one to which we will refer in this book, even though only about five percent of his manuscript concerns raised gilding, while the bulk is devoted to the techniques of fresco and tempera painting. And though his work is less clearly written, the unknown De Arte author provides a valuable perspective on the status of the illuminator at this time in history. The De Arte author confines himself exclusively to a discussion of the techniques of the illuminator, distinguishing them from the techniques of either the scribe or the painter. Today, these distinctions are largely unrecognized, and the person who practices illumination/gilding doubtlessly performs his own lettering and may also perform his own painting and design of his work. Therefore, he is likely to regard himself as scribe, illuminator, and painter, more or less. But the De Arte author received his manuscript after it had already been written by someone else. And though he might write out a chapter heading, he was not a scribe; and though he might ornament his page or execute miniature paintings on it, he was not a painter. What he was was decorator of written books, an unknown profession today, and one whose distinctness may even have been less clear in the thirteenth or fifteenth centuries. But in the fourteenth century, gilding, which lives in a middle ground between decorative writing and painting, was enjoying its moment in the sun, as an art professionally independent of either of the other two. It was with confidence, then, that the author of De Arte Illuminati could write an entire book dealing solely with the techniques of illumination, and know that there were those eager to learn and follow them (De Arte, XI-XII).

For all of that, it is still in Cennini's manuscript that we find the clearest information on gilding techniques. And yet almost nobody returns to the translations of Cennini for his information. Instead, a gilder will purchase a contemporary work which provides him, ostensibly, with Cennini's information in modern language and modern techniques perhaps not discovered in the fourteenth century. This only makes sense, yet a problem has arisen as the information has been handed down from one writer to another. Certain of Cennini's methods have been ignored, overlooked or lost in that precarious passage through the years, and the result is that all current works on gilding are unworkable in one or more crucial areas. If I was to write out the rules of a game, say baseball, but fail to put them in any kind of sequence, rather simply write them out at random; the users of those rules would have difficulty playing the game as we know it, and their version would only coincide with the proper method of play by chance, and infrequently.

The same likelihood of success can be expected from gilding techniques currently available to the public. The flaws in these techniques stem from misreadings of Cennini's recipe for making gesso, by early practitioners, such as Graily Hewitt. Gilding, as the chapter titles in this book suggest, is a three step process: preparing gesso, applying the gesso, and applying gold. Attempting to gild without having a proper gesso is something akin to trying to play baseball without a bat: you can still play, but why bother. In fairness to Hewitt, Cennini's gesso recipe and the method of preparing it do not provide the precise instructions of the modern cookbook, such as: cook in conventional oven at 450°F. for 30 minutes; melt 1/4 cup unsalted butter; mince 1/2 cup fresh basil leaves. Instead, Cennini is about as clear as a native giving directions to a tourist: follow the forked road into town and look for the small house (il Libro, 100). Yet their misreadings of Cennini have spawned the recent inaccuracies of others such as Irene Base, who takes her recipe from Hewitt, and of Donald Jackson, who takes his own recipe from Base. It is Jackson who is the most recent major source for gilding techniques.

I will not pursue here the specific nature of these flaws until the next section describing the preparation of the gesso. It is enough to say that by a flawed recipe I mean a recipe which yields a workable gesso only sometimes, far less than half the time. I know that these recipes are flawed because I have used them many times myself, and any experienced gilder who has used them will tell you the same thing. What is more, you need only compare the amount of space each of these writers allows for explaining how to make the gesso with the space allowed for what to do when it doesn't work, to discover that their methods are far from precise. Most of them have a journeyman car mechanic's attitude toward their procedures: (Did you check the spark plugs? The battery? When's the last time you changed the oil?) They assume things will go wrong, and then tell you how you might remedy the problem. Hewitt's attitude is even less professional than the mechanic's, and he cautions that the gesso recipe he offers may fail you because the eggs you use to acquire egg whites for the recipe come from different chickens than those in Cennini's time, and so "we are uncertain...as to the powers of our hens in comparison with his, for so domestic a bird has probably undergone ungaugeable, however slight, chemical evolution since his day" (Hewitt, 281).

It is this inability to exercise control of their craft at the crucial stage of preparing a workable gesso which has hampered modern gilders. The techniques I offer here are not simply another version of a misreading of Cennini; but are, instead, the first version of the proper reading of Cennini, and the first workable modern techniques to appear in print. By workable, I mean that if followed accurately, my gesso recipe works every time. This is a claim no previous writer on gilding can make without lying. I know my recipe works every time because I use it frequently, as have my students. But for those of you frustrated by only occasional success in gilding, and for those of you new to the craft, the proof of what I say is in the doing of it.

Chapter One:
Preparing the Gesso

Materials Required for this Section:

White Lead powder
Granulated Table Sugar
Hide Glue
Slaked Plaster of Paris
Armenian Bole Powder
Distilled Water

Two Mixing Bowls
Rubber Spatula
Basic Measuring Tools for Liquids and Powders, eg. Tablespoon, teaspoon, Graduated measuring cup

Definition and Use

Gesso is made from the materials listed above. Though the term itself has a variety of meanings, we use it here in the sense most often used by gilders, as a thick paint or paste which, when dry, provides a raised surface upon which gold is applied. In raised gilding, gesso functions as both an adhesive for the gold, as well as its pillow or platform. Gesso's function as a platform distinguishes it from other binders such as gum arabic or honey mixtures or glues which are used, for example, to perform flat gilding. Because gold has traditionally been regarded as the brightest material which also possesses malleable qualities, it has long been reserved for illustrating the most valued manuscripts. And as platforms are built so that we might better view the speakers and entertainers who stand on them, so the gesso is a kind of stage which heightens the drama of the gold performing on it. On the flat terrain of the page, the gilded object is a prince, but the object raised by the gesso and then gilded is a king.

Formula for Making Gesso

Like the techniques of gilding, the formula for making gesso comes from Cennini. His formula reads as follows:

If you want to do illuminating...you will need to have some of a color, or rather a gesso, which is called size, and is made as follows: take a little gesso sottile, and a small amount of white lead, less than a third as much as of the gesso; then take a little sugar candy, less than the white lead. Grind these things very fine with clear water. Then scrape it up; and let it dry without sun (Craftsman's, 100).

As I have mentioned, while his formula is the most clearly written of those available from medieval times, it is still rather vague. Yet it is not Cennini's vague language that led the early gilding revivalists astray, but rather their own failure to recognize certain specific terms among his otherwise general terminology. Their mistakes were duplicated by later gilding experts, who either failed themselves to spot the key items in Cennini or simply accepted the mistaken formula they were handed without even realizing it was faulty. And today, veteran and novice gilders alike employ a version of this flawed formula when making their own gesso. They accept the hack mechanic's hit and miss approach, and the frustration incumbent upon such an approach as simply part of the difficulty of the craft. And why shouldn't they, since this is what the experts tell them to do. Refusing advice from a gilding luminary such as Donald Jackson would be like one of our novice ballplayers refusing to accept hitting instruction from Henry Aaron. You just don't do it.

But in this case you do, and the reason why comprises a fascinating footnote not only to gilding but perhaps even to history itself. The reason why involves us with Mr. Graily Hewitt, who is to gilding what Abner Doubleday is to baseball.

Hewitt and his gilding techniques rose to prominence following England's rather recent recognition of gilding as an art worthy of great prestige. England's knowledge of gilding dates from Lady Merryfield's first English translation of Cennini in 1824. But it was not until William Morris and others read these translations of Cennini's techniques and produced their own gilded works, that gilding can be said to have truly been re-born after a five hundred year death. And England readily accepted this bright child as one of her own. Suddenly, gesso formulas abounded, and everyone seemed to have his own homemade best, like everyone has the best recipe for chili or chicken soup. Later still, art supply houses began selling already made mixes they called gessos, but which were in many cases materials entirely different from Cennini's gesso.

It was in the midst of this gilding renaissance that Graily Hewitt interposed his Lettering, which contained the first complete treatise on gilding since Cennini's manuscripts. Though Hewitt frequently acknowledges his reliance upon the medieval work, his own instruction is considerably different from Cennini's. As a result, Hewitt's techniques superseded Cennini's, and have become the hallmark for gilders since. And so, we find later writers on gilding, such as Irene Base, crediting Hewitt with reviving the practice of gilding, a well as acknowledging reliance upon his work to formulate her own (96). And in his turn, Donald Jackson, scribe to the Queen of England, doffs his cap to both Base and Hewitt(183). With Jackson as their most esteemed practitioner, we can say that Hewitt's techniques have survived nearly unchanged form his time to ours.

It is chiefly to Graily Hewitt, then, that we owe our modern gilding techniques. Yet I have said that these widely accepted techniques, particularly those for preparing gesso, are deeply flawed, and that my own are superior. Having provided this background, it is time to demonstrate what I say.

In chapter 28 of his book, Hewitt explains how to make gesso by way of referring constantly to the Cennini recipe. But Hewitt is more concerned with undermining Cennini's formula than with explaining how to use it. He complains that when Cennini says to finely grind the gesso sottile with the sugar, the lead, and the water, that we can't be sure how finely he means for us to grind; that when he says to use sugar candy we can't be sure what kind he means; that when he says to temper the mixture with egg white we can't be sure the eggs our hens lay have the same chemical composition as those laid by his hens (Hewitt 280-281). Entwined with Hewitt's complaints are his own minor variations upon Cennini's recipe, plus the single major variation, the inclusion of fish glue, which he recommends in place of some of the excessive amount of sugar he claims appears in Cennini's formula (Hewitt 282).

Hewitt's objective is clearly to destroy Cennini's formula, and erect his own in its place. How else can we explain the shrillness of such complaints, or the absurdity of his recommending the use of fish glue in place of some of the sugar, as if Cennini's formula contained no glue; as if Hewitt himself was the first to suggest using glue for a gesso. In fact, Cennini suggests several uses for fish glue, but the making of a gesso for gilding is not among them (Thompson, De Arte 30). Instead, Cennini and the other principle gilders of his time, preferred hide glue - parchment size - made from the clippings or scrapings of animal skins (Thompson De Arte 30). They believed that the affinity among the materials enabled them to function more effectively, and some gilders even took the trouble of making their size from the very same skin upon which they planned to gild (Thompson, materials 59). However, Hewitt's advocating fish rather than hide size is not the issue so much as his apparent presumption that he was the first to recommend it, as if all Cennini used for an adhesive was sugar.

Now anyone beyond the level of novice knows that sugar itself is not a sufficient binder, that its function in fact, is not to bind, but to make the gesso somewhat pliable, and less susceptible to cracking when dry. Surely Graily Hewitt knew all this also, and knew that Cennini knew it, too. Yet Hewitt never alludes to Cennini's use of a size and if we examine Cennini's formula for gesso printed above, we find that he makes no mention of adding size. Was Hewitt right? Could Cennini, a master craftsman, have forgotten or somehow failed to include size in his gesso recipe, a mistake equivalent to forgetting chocolate in a chocolate cake recipe? The answer is emphatically no, and we can prove it with the certainty that a fingerprint proves identity.

The proof is in Cennini's formula itself, and resides in the apparently innocuous yet curious instruction "let it dry without sun", referring to what you do with the gesso once all the ingredients are mixed. Why would Cennini want his gesso to dry out of the sun, when we typically place things in the sun so that its heat will dry them faster? The only reason he would provide such a precise instruction would be if his gesso contained size or glue, substances which will not dry in the heat of the sun. And while he does not actually mention either the words "size" or "glue" in his formula, it is still clearly present. For when Cennini listed gesso sottile as his first ingredient, he assumed that his readers knew that gesso sottile already contained size in it; that to list size as a separate ingredient would be redundant, confusing, and plainly incorrect; akin, perhaps, to instructing someone to pack a suitcase with clothes, and also to pack another suitcase inside the first one (Thompson, De Arte 49).

While Cennini's assumption is obviously foreign to modern gilders, it was common practice then, as Thompson points out: "almost invariably size was mixed with the gesso grosso, with the gesso sottile always" (Il Libro, 233). Yet it is this taken for granted aspect of preparing a gesso which we should be familiar with, crucial as it is to preparing a consistent, workable gesso rather than one that requires constant doctoring. After all, I use almost precisely the same kinds of ingredients as Hewitt, Base, Jackson, and others use. It is, rather, the manner in which I combine these ingredients that makes the difference. Two people, for example might make bread using the same ingredients: but while one simply mixes the ingredients, forms them into a loaf, and bakes it; the other allows the mixture to rise, punches it down, and allows it to rise again before baking it. Their resulting loaves will be dramatically different, the one a dense as clay, the other porous as a honeycomb.

I make my gesso in not one, but two distinct stages. In the first stage, I combine only these ingredients: the slaked plaster of Paris, the size, and the water. I mix them together, and allow the mixture to dry. Chemically speaking, this dried substance possesses a remarkable tenacity that can, at first, only be perceived under a microscope. Analysis reveals that in my dried part one mixture, or in what Cennini called gesso sottile, the size adheres to, or lines up with the needle - like plaster of Paris formations. On the other hand, analysis of a completed single stage gesso, of the type anyone who followed the conventional Hewitt and progeny method would produce; the very gesso that nearly all gilders today make and are frustrated by; this analysis reveals that the size neither adheres to the needles of slaked plaster, nor is it distributed uniformly about the material. Rather, it appears in amorphous random globs. It is this uncertain distribution of the size that requires Hewitt, Base, and others to make odd suggestions such as cutting the dried gesso like you would cut a slice "out of a jam sandwich," that is, from the center to the edge and from top to bottom, so "that one may rely upon having the due preparation of the ingredients" (Hewitt, 287). They learned from experience that some of the gesso from a given mix would hold the leaf while some wouldn't. They hoped that by cutting a jam sandwich slice, they could get a little gesso from each part of their dried cake, and have a better chance of finding some size in the slice. But this jam sandwich method remained a crap shoot at best because the simple fact was that they didn't know where their size was located. The uncertainty is eliminated in my two stage process. The microscopic analysis illustrates that a two stage process has the great advantage of allowing the size to mix evenly with the plaster, and to lock permanently onto it in a chemical bond which the imposition of other ingredients or of grinding cannot destroy. No such bond can form when all the ingredients are mixed in one stage.

      Six hundred years ago, in Italy's artistic flowering, every artist knew that slaked plaster of Paris was always mixed with size prior to being mixed with anything else; just as anyone who has baked a cake knows that you don't mix the ingredients for the cake with those for the frosting, and then bake. They are made in two distinct steps, a fact so obvious that recipe writers don't mention it, just as Cennini didn't mention what was already understood.

Five hundred years later, Graily Hewitt ushered in the era of modern gilding by trying to bake a cake in one step; and ridiculous as that is, everyone after him did the same thing. All my formula does is bake the cake in two steps, the way it was meant to be done. And though many gilders have fretted over their unworkable gessos, it is remarkable to think that it's taken us six hundred years to figure out what was always there. If not for the simple recognition of what the two words, "without sun" suggest, who's to say how much longer Graily Hewitt would have gotten away with playing follow the leader.

Before discussing the formula itself, I must emphasize that it is not an approximation, but a precise series of proportions and processes. This is not preparation by taste, but by strict adherence to a proven method. Unlike others, who suggest adding "sticky matter" or "toughening matter" when the gold doesn't adhere, or when the gesso crumbles, no additions to my formula are required (Johnston 128).

Again, the materials I use in my formula are basically the same as those used by Cennini, and others after him. And again, while they strayed from his order of preparation, I have not. And as we said earlier, we might provide a group of novices with the ten basic rules of baseball, and then set them loose in a field to try their luck. But unless we explained the order in which these rules should be applied, and therefore the connections between them, what they did on that field probably wouldn't look much like baseball.

My formula for gesso is prepared in two distinct stages or parts, as follows:

Part One

In a mixing bowl, combine the following ingredients:

8 parts slaked Plaster of Paris
1 part hide glue
2 parts distilled water

By "parts" I mean whatever unit of measurement you choose to use, and will depend upon how much gesso you want to make. For example, if your unit of measure is a tablespoon, you would combine eight tablespoons of slaked Plaster of Paris, with one tablespoon of glue, with two tablespoons water. You should be aware that gesso stretches quite a long way when it comes time to reconstituting it with water and applying it to the page. But, just how far it stretches varies greatly according to how thick you make your gesso when reconstituting it, as well as how high you choose to raise your letter off the page.

Stir the ingredients with a rubber spatula until you get a smooth, off-white substance. Allow this material to dry in the same bowl in a cool, dry place, away from the sun or other heat source. Removing it to another container might slightly upset the proportion between the materials. It will require two to three days for the water to evaporate. When it does, you are left with the substance Cennini referred to as gesso sottile with size. This mixture becomes fully concentrated once the water has been evaporated. A complete bonding has now occurred. Set the mixture aside, and proceed with part two of the formula.

Part Two

In a smaller bowl, combine the following ingredients:

3 parts white lead powder
1 part sugar
2 parts distilled water
pinch (size of a match-head) Armenian Bole

Again, for "parts", use the same unit of measurement used for Part One. In a smaller mixing bowl, first combine the sugar with the water, and make a solution. Then add the white lead and the Armenian Bole, and stir all the ingredients together. Add this mixture to the bowl in which your Part One mixture, your gesso sottile, has now dried. Wait ten minutes for the liquid to settle into the dry mixture, then stir the two together.

Your gesso is now completed and only requires time to dry before it is ready for use. Allow it to dry in the open air for one to seven days, either in the same bowl you mixed it in, or by pouring it into smaller containers if you find them more convenient. The length of the drying depends upon the variables of temperature and humidity in the room where you're drying it: cooler, dryer conditions will enhance the drying process.

To determine if your gesso is completely dry and ready to use, you can cut or break off a piece of it; and if it is dry within as well as without then it's ready. If it isn't entirely dry you should wait, because a sticky gesso will not reconstitute into a smooth, workable paint, but will remain gummy and difficult to use.

When your gesso is completely dry and ready to use, you can scrape off what you'll need, grind it into a granulated state, and reconstitute it with water. We'll discuss reconstituting in the next section dealing with the application of gesso. For the moment, I suggest that you grind your now bowl-shaped chunk of gesso into granules, which are easier to store, to measure, and to reconstitute with water. You can grind the gesso using an electric coffee grinder, a simple hand coffee grinder set at a coarse setting or a mortar and pestle. Either way, granules are the best state in which to work with the gesso, even better than powder, which tends to remain too thick when reconstituted. Once you've ground your gesso, it is best to store it in a dry, airtight container in a cool place, so that it doesn't acquire moisture.

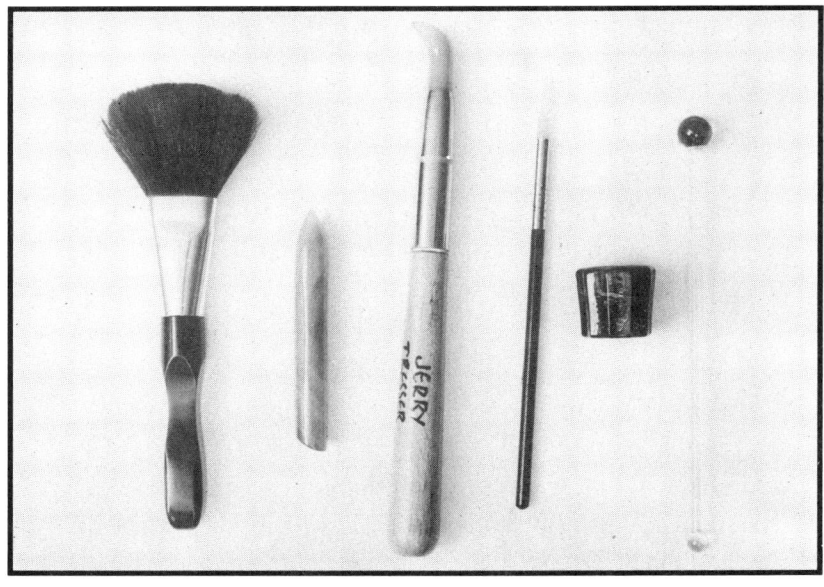

From left to right, Gilders mop brush, Solid agate burnisher, Dogs tooth agate, Pointed agate, Dappen dish and rod.

Chapter Two:
Applying the Gesso

Materials Required for This Section:
Dappen dish, or equivalent deep-dished glass or china container
Glass-headed mixing rod
Crow quill pen, size #513EF
Small paint brushes, sizes #00, 0, 1
Glassine paper
Agate burnisher
Egg whites
Distilled water

Reconstituting

This is the first step toward the application itself. You will need to measure out the amount of gesso you want, using, for example, fractional teaspoon measurements. I mix one eighth teaspoon of gesso with five drops of distilled water in a Dappen dish, cover it, and allow it to sit undisturbed for an hour. This combination of gesso to water is purely a matter of personal taste. These combinations produce for me a fairly thin, free-flowing gesso which I find easy to use. You may want to alter the consistency by using less or more water, but bear in mind that contrary to the advice of many gilding notables, gesso should not ordinarily be applied in one thick coat, but in several thinner coats (cf. Jackson 183, Johnston 114). We will discuss the reason for this shortly.

Before we proceed, I want to draw attention also to the importance of working with small amounts of gesso in small, deep dishes. This is in order to more easily control the quick drying property of the gesso, which would dry to the sides of a larger, shallower dish.

Application

While you are waiting for the gesso to mix with the water, you may want to outline the figures or letters you plan to gild, using a pencil so that you can erase any drawing errors you might make.

To begin applying the gesso, dip your quill or brush into the prepared mixture taking only a small amount until you become accustomed to its properties. As you apply it, work generally from the edge of the figure toward the center, pulling the gesso with your instrument always toward the inside of the figure. This will prevent the gesso from seeping beyond the edges. You will need to work rather quickly, keeping in mind that the gesso begins to dry about nine seconds after it has been applied.

While you will naturally want your initial application to be precise, you do not need to worry about mistakes, or about later alterations, as long as you bear in mind that the application process should be regarded as a gradual additive procedure. We might compare it to the procedure that a haircutter would follow with a client who was unsure just how short she wanted her hair to be cut: rather than begin by chopping off a large amount of hair, he would cut only a small amount off and allow the client to decide if she was satisfied or wanted more cut. Thus, after you have made your first application you might find for example, that the letters of a given word are not of a uniform height, and that you will need to add gesso to some of them in order to even them out.

To do this, you will need to interface the already applied gesso with that you are about to apply on top of it. In order to receive this second layer of gesso the first layer must be moistened with water brushed onto it, otherwise the new second layer would not adhere to the dry first layer. Once you've moistened the first layer you can apply the second in the same way already described. Applying a second layer allows you to not only make changes in the height of letters, but to remove bubbles, scrapes, or other blemishes. You can continue to apply new layers of gesso to your figures as long as you interface the old and new layers, and as long as the previous layer is completely dry. Drying time is usually about twenty-four hours. Again, however, this sort of control over your gesso application is only possible if you are using a fairly thin gesso since even the second layer of a thick gesso might be more than you want.

This additive process gives you far more control than those methods which suggest, for example, that you scrape the gesso off of your figures to even them out. In the event that you do go outside of the borders of your figures, you can remove the excess gesso by first allowing it to dry completely, and then scraping it carefully away with the blade of a knife, taking care not to cut your vellum in the process.

The amount of gesso to apply to your figures is again, a matter of taste, and will depend upon how high you want your figures raised off the page. You should bear in mind, however, what I call the dome theory, and that is the bubbling effect that the liquid gesso, in addition to the water used for interfacing, will cause on the surface of the vellum or paper as it dries. This natural convexity of the surface produces its own raised effect quite independent of the raised effect obtained by layering the gesso. In fact, when gilding was first practiced the raised effect was not intended, and was only achieved accidentally as a result of the natural bubbling of the vellum. The effect was pleasing and so the techniques were maintained. (Thompson, Materials and Techniques, 208).

Using Glair

Glair is what I refer to as an external size, as opposed to the internal size already in the gesso, and though Cennini suggests using it, it is not necessary because the gesso prepared by the methods here is a strong enough mordant by itself. Cennini may have suggested it simply as a precautionary measure to insure the gesso's stickiness.

However, glair is a valuable material when you are gilding a very small space: that is, when the surface area is small, and the gesso must be applied in a single step. In this case the glair adds an extra kick to the gesso's mordant quality.

To prepare glair, beat an egg white until it is stiff, and then let it sit overnight at room temperature. In the morning, separate the liquid from the froth, and mix the liquid only with an equal amount of distilled water. This is glair, and you can use it in place of water when reconstituting the gesso. You should bear in mind, however, that glair is a waterproofing material, and that gesso reconstituted with it must be gilded upon while still slightly damp, that is, after twenty-four hours. Otherwise, if the gesso is allowed to dry completely, the breathing process performed to soften it just prior to applying the gold leaf will be ineffective. On the other hand, gesso reconstituted with water alone should, as indicated above, be allowed to dry for at least twenty-four hours, and may be allowed to sit almost indefinitely before the gold is applied.

Polishing

Prior to burnishing, additional surface imperfections such as bubbled or uneven patches may be removed by interfacing new gesso onto old using water and a small paint brush. Allow these touched up areas to dry as directed before. The purpose of polishing the gesso prior to applying the gold leaf is to provide the smoothest possible surface on which to lay the leaf. Even though the leaf is opaque gold, its ultra-thinness renders it nearly translucent to textures. Surface flaws on the gesso cannot, of course, be removed once the leaf is applied. Additionally, the leaf adheres more readily to a smooth rather than a rough surface.

To polish the gesso you will need an agate burnisher, and a glassine paper to protect the gesso from being nicked by the burnisher in the event it is not quite dry. Cover the gesso with the paper, and rub the burnisher firmly back and forth over the gesso surface. When you are certain that the gesso is completely dry you may polish directly onto it without using the paper. At this point, the gesso can withstand nearly any degree of pressure.

Chapter Three:
Applying the Gold

Materials Required for This Section:
Gilder's Mop Brush
Standard Weight Patent Gold   #4 or #5 pencil
Standard Weight Transfer Gold   Reverse tweezers
Scissors   Gilder's Tip
Reed Breathing Tube   Gilder's Knife
Glassine Paper   Gilder's Cushion
16 lb. Bond Paper   Utility Knife
Small Paint Brush   Hematite Burnisher

A Provision Prior to Application

Prior to applying gold to the gesso, I hasten to remind you that once the gold is applied it cannot be removed except by damaging the gesso. Thus, you should polish your gesso until the surface is as smooth as glass. The way the surface of the gesso looks is, effectively, the way the surface of the leaf will look once it's applied. This smooth surface will prevent the delicate leaf from being nicked by a rough blemish, will offer an optimally adherent medium for the leaf, and will enhance its brilliance once it's applied.

A Note About Gold

While gold is available in a variety of thicknesses and degrees of purity, I recommend that you use standard, single weight patent gold with a purity of twenty-two karats. This quality of gold is the most workable, effective, and economic form to use when performing raised gilding. A more complete discussion of gold varieties and their uses may be found in the glossary.

Application

Since you must again reconstitute the gesso, this time by means of the moisture in your breath, you must also, as you did before, work quickly within the constraints imposed by its quick-drying characteristic. However, since you are now only moistening its surface to receive the gold, its hygroscopicity will cause it to dry even more quickly than before, in about three seconds. Thus, all your materials must be ready at hand before you blow on the gesso. To prepare, you should place your gessoed figures on a flat, hard surface. Next, you should decide how many figures to work on at the same time. When you've acquired some proficiency with the procedures you can work with several figures at once, but initially I would suggest applying the gold to just once figure at a time.

Now you must cut your patent gold in accordance with the size of the object to be covered. To do this, remove one leaf at a time from the book, and cut the leaf so that it is slightly larger than the object to be covered. In this way you can be sure to completely cover your object with the leaf in the first application. The small amount of leaf wasted in this overlap method is well worth it in view of the effort you save by not needing to repeat the process simply to cover a small spot. You will want to cut several pieces of approximately the same size, the idea being to add as much gold as the figure will hold. Cutting the leaf is as simple as cutting a piece of paper, and can be done with a pair of clean, sharp scissors.

You are now ready to apply the leaf. But before you proceed, make certain that you have a piece of glassine paper, and a burnisher of any type within reach on your work table. Pick up your first leaf with the reverse tweezers, and lay it nearby. Since the tweezers clamp the gold without continual pressure from your hand, they allow you to work more freely. Place the additional pieces of leaf on the edge of a book, for example, or other small, raised surface, so that you can easily grasp them. Now, place the reed breathing tube between your lips, and, if you are right-handed, hold the tweezers in that hand, leaving your left hand free. I use a reed tube because it absorbs any excess moisture accumulating as I breath on the figures. Aim the tube at your object, just an inch or two above it, and exhale strongly through the tube, allowing your breath to cover the entire object. Immediately place the leaf on top of the figure, release the tweezers, and press the leaf onto the entire figure with the left hand, applying a pressure sufficient simply to allow it to adhere to the sticky surface without damaging it. Quickly top the leaf with the glassine paper, and, holding it in place with your left hand, apply a brief but firm burnish to the object, simply to secure the leaf onto the gesso. Then, remove the glassine, and peel away the leaf's tissue backing. Pick up another leaf with the tweezers, and repeat the procedure until you find that the gold is no longer adhering to the surface. The purpose of adding gold on top of gold even in areas that have already been covered is to obtain a deeper color and shine when the object is burnished.

After you've completed these procedures, you may find that small areas remain uncovered, particularly along the edges or joints of the figure. To cover these small areas you will now need the 16 lb. bond paper and the #4 or #5H pencil close at hand. Using a small piece of leaf, repeat the procedure, only this time once you've pressed the leaf onto the gesso, cover it with the bond paper, and press it into the edge or corner of the object by rubbing the point of the pencil along the edge. Then, remove the bond paper and peel away the leaf's tissue backing, as before.

Burnishing

Once you have determined that your object can take no more gold, and that complete coverage has been obtained, you are ready for the final step in the gilding process, the burnishing of the gold. You should wait, however, at least a few hours after you've applied the gold to do any burnishing, and even the burnishing you will now do is a kind of testing of the quality of your gold coverage. This waiting time allows the gold leaf to securely adhere to the gesso, and allows the gesso to dry so that it will not be damaged by the pressure applied during the burnishing process.

You perform this preliminary burnishing on a hard table top using glassine paper, and a hematite or psilomelanite burnisher. Hematite is always preferred. Take a small square of the glassine paper, cover the object with it, and, while holding it down with one hand, rub the side of the burnisher lightly over the surface of the object with your other hand. You will find that you can use any of the surfaces of the burnisher for general burnishing, while the point works well for corners and edges. The purpose of this burnishing through the glassine paper is to discover any uneven areas on the surface of your object, that is, small spots where the gold might not have adhered or where less gold adhered than adhered to the rest of your object. After the rubbing you perform, these spots will appear as dark patches on the glassine paper, the paper functioning in the manner of an x-ray picture which also points out spots or irregularities. Before you perform direct burnishing you will want to cover these uneven spots by adding more gold in the manner I've described.

After twenty-four hours the object is dry enough to withstand direct burnishing. At this point you will want to switch both the surface you are burnishing on, as well as the burnisher itself. Ideally, you will want to burnish on top of a cold surface, such as an aluminum plate which has been refrigerated, or a slab of marble. In conjunction with this cold surface, you should use a true hematite burnisher, also known as a bloodstone. The hematite is a hot burnisher, which means it generates heat as you rub it across the surface of your object. This heat, when combined with the cold surface beneath, serves to eliminate any excess dampness in the gesso, while forging the gesso and gold into a lasting union.

At this stage, you will begin by again burnishing through the glassine paper, though this time the purpose of this indirect burnishing is to test the hardness of the gesso. While the gesso will most likely be completely dry, the paper buffer will allow you an added precaution. Hold the paper and burnisher in the same manner as before, and apply increasing pressure onto the surface of the object, feeling for any give or tenderness or stickiness to the gesso. When you are confident that the gesso is dry, you can burnish directly onto the surface of the gold, applying at least as much pressure as you did when polishing the gesso itself earlier. The medieval masters, for example, spoke of burnishing so hard that sweat stood out on their brows. Continue burnishing with this steady pressure until you feel the object has attained a shine that you're happy with.

The gilding process is now complete, and you are left only with the task of removing any excess gesso or gold on the gilding surface. You can do this by dusting the area with a gilder's mop, or by gently scraping away excess materials with the edge of a knife, taking care not to cut the gilding surface. If you are not going to display your work immediately, you can safely store it in a cool, dry place by covering the surface with a piece of tissue paper, and by placing the entire work between pieces of cardboard or other firm, flat surface.

Applying Transfer Gold

If, for some reason, you are unable obtain sufficient coverage with patent gold using the techniques I've described, you may resort to using transfer gold. Transfer gold is the only form in which gold was once produced. It is more difficult to work with, requires additional tools, but in certain situations you can accomplish with it what you cannot accomplish with patent gold. This is because you will now need to moisten your gesso not simply with your breath, but with water brushed or dabbed onto the uncovered areas with a soft brush. When the gesso is this wet, it becomes too soft to use the patent gold on it because the pressure needed to apply the patent gold to the gesso might damage the surface of the gesso. It is here that transfer gold is essential, because it can simply be dropped rather than pressed onto the wet gesso.

To work with transfer gold you will need a gilder's cushion, a gilder's tip, and a gilder's knife. With the cushion in front of you on the table, the easiest way to remove a leaf of gold from the book is to open it to the first leaf, and quickly flip the book over, pressing it flatly onto the cushion, as you would a pancake in the pan. This should prevent the leaf from straying off the cushion. If the leaf is not laying quite flat on the cushion, you can smooth it out by carefully running the blunt edge of the gilder's knife beneath it, picking it up on the blade, gently shaking out the creases, and then rolling or laying it out again on the cushion. You may also find it helpful to blow gently into the center of the leaf to remove the creases. Bear in mind, however, that handling the leaf at all will require some practice because it is as light as a feather, yet considerably larger and more delicate.

Once the leaf is flat on the cushion, you will want to cut the appropriate sized piece to amply cover the exposed surface. To cut the leaf, bring the gilder's knife directly down onto the leaf, and then saw it back and forth with firm, but not heavy pressure. As you cut, make certain that the tip of the knife remains extended beyond the far edge of the leaf, to prevent it from nicking the leaf, and possibly causing it to tear or twist.

You are ready now to place the cut gold onto the gesso. Wet the gesso lightly using a brush and water, but try not to wet the surrounding area where you have already applied gold. To pick up the gold off the cushion, take the gilder's tip, and run the bristles through your hair a few times so that they acquire a bit of oil. Then hold the tip just above the piece of gold, and parallel with its surface. Now press the tip firmly down onto the gold and lift it off the cushion. Next, bring the tip with the gold directly over the spot where you want to apply it, and then press it quickly and lightly onto the wet gesso and remove it just as quickly. This press and remove process should be accomplished in one smooth movement. Once you have achieved coverage with the transfer gold, you can add patent gold on top without interfacing because gold adheres well to itself. Allow the gesso to dry for twenty-four hours, and burnish as before. Any wrinkles in the gold as it lays on the wet surface will be removed by the hard burnishing you perform later.

Additional Notes

While I recommend that you apply gold to one object at a time until you are acquainted with the procedures, I do suggest that you burnish all of the objects, or at least many of them, at the same time. This is only dictated by common sense, since you must wait twenty-four hours to gild at all, and since the procedure and tools for applying and for burnishing are entirely different. This suggestion is contingent on the number and size of the objects you're gilding but a general rule is to apply gold to half your figures on one day; burnish them on the second day, and also apply gold to the other figures; and then burnish these other figures on the third day.

Special Preparations:
Slaking Plaster of Paris

Plaster of Paris, or gypsum, was originally mined in various parts of southern Europe. In its natural state it is yellow, and crystalline in structure. Craftsmen burned the gypsum to remove impurities that accompanied it from the quarries. Burning caused it to turn white and to lose all of its water. This form of gypsum is called gesso grosso. What slaking does it simply put the water lost in the burning process, back into the gypsum. Thus, the mineral has an initial crystalline formation, which becomes amorphous upon burning, but which is returned to its crystalline form when slaked. The term for this process is called calcination.

Slaking originally required thirty days to perform during which time the unslaked Plaster of Paris, or gypsum, combined with the water to form the new material called gesso sottile, or slaked Plaster of Paris; and also during this time the gypsum's impurities were removed. In the original process, a pound of gypsum was combined with about one and a half gallons of water, and the mixture was stirred with great vigor for one half hour, then allowed to sit overnight. The next day the cloudy water was poured off, replaced by clean water, and the process was repeated. This rather daunting procedure was repeated over and again for thirty days, at which time the water sitting with the gesso remained clear, and the gesso was deemed slaked and ready for use in raised gilding.

While it is reasonable to imagine performing such a process in Cennini's time, it is difficult, in this age of the two minute cake, to seriously consider spending thirty days even before you begin to gild. Yet prior to this book, any gilding manual you might consult, whether past or current, will explain how to slake by the same ancient method Cennini used. I have developed a simple procedure which allows you to slake not in thirty days, but in thirty minutes.

Before I discuss this procedure, let me refer to the conventional method, and explain just exactly what it does. It is during the initial thirty minutes of vigorous stirring that the gypsum combines with the water, re-crystallizing its form, and becoming the same substance - minus impurities - that it originally was, the substance we call slaked Plaster of Paris. The remaining twenty-nine days of stirring accomplished absolutely nothing in regard to slaking, the value being in the purification of the plaster occurring as a result of the daily changing of the water. Cennini didn't realize that he probably could have achieved this slaked quality earlier anymore than today's gilders do. Cennini judged that his plaster was slaked when the water he mixed with it finally remained clear, and when it felt silky smooth, the same signs today's gilders look for.

To slake plaster in thirty minutes rather than thirty days, you will need, in addition to unslaked plaster and distilled water, a pH kit which you can purchase at a swimming pool supply store. You can use either the liquid form of the kit, or the kit which contains pH strips. Understand that unslaked plaster is acidic, while slaked plaster - like distilled water - is neutral, that is, it has a pH of seven. Thus, when your plaster reaches a pH of seven you know that it is slaked.

Take a small amount of the unslaked plaster, say four ounces, so that you can stir it easily, and mix it in a bowl with about sixteen ounces of distilled water. The water should have a neutral pH, but check it with your testing material just to be sure prior to mixing it with the plaster. Stir the mixture vigorously for about three minutes, allow the plaster to settle in the container, then test the pH of the water again. You will notice that the liquid has become less acidic, that is, it is moving across the color chart from yellow toward blue. Repeat these steps until a neutral pH reading is obtained. When your mixture tests neutral, your plaster is both slaked and pure, and, at this point, no matter how much water you might add, the mixture will get no purer than a pH of seven. Allow it to dry in the bowl, and then grind it down to store in powder form for later use.

While Cennini knew that his plaster was slaked when the water mixed with it remained clear, we know that ours is slaked when its pH reading is neutral. Of course, we can acquire plaster that is much purer than what Cennini had access to, and thus, the purification process of changing the water requires only a few minutes, rather than a month. Nevertheless, the real key to the brevity of my procedure lies in the simple pH testing process, and the simple knowledge that slaked plaster is achieved within the first thirty minutes of stirring and changing the water. This will doubtlessly come as a shocking bit of information to contemporary gilding experts and their followers practicing the thirty day method. In fact, many experts, while unaware of the thirty minute process, aren't even sure about their own thirty day process: "Refill the pail with fresh water, stir it for ten minutes or so, and repeat this process every day for a week. After that, every other day for at least four more weeks [I would say three]" (Handbook II, 184, Jackson).

Hide Glue

To prepare hide glue, accurately referred to as hide or parchment size, you will need to obtain four ounces of parchment clippings or scrapings. Additionally, you will need a glass jar, and a metal strainer.

Pour two pints of water into a pot and bring the water to a boil. Lower the temperature to simmer, and throw the clippings into the pot. Allow them to simmer for one and one half hours, or until about half of the water has evaporated. Strain the remaining liquid into a jar, and allow the liquid to settle at room temperature, until it acquires a jelly-like consistency. This jelly should be well covered in the jar and refrigerated, and may be kept indefinitely in the refrigerator until ready for use.

When you are ready to prepare gesso sottile according to the methods described earlier, cut off a piece of this now hardened glue, and place it in an already warm double boiler. Allow the glue to liquefy, but not boil else its binding capability will be destroyed. Take whatever portion of this now liquid size you need, and combine it with the gesso according to the proportions described earlier.

This kind of glue is almost pure Gelatin, very soluble in water and maintains a tenacious bond when mixed with gesso sottile. Traditionally it was the only size used, and while today it is available in certain art supply stores, it is not nearly so pure or effective as the kind acquired by making it yourself. Hide glue remains the best glue available for performing raised gilding, particularly when velum is the surface you are gilding on. As I have mentioned, the medieval masters recognized that like materials performed best in conjunction with each other and so hide glue was nearly always used when gilding on vellum.

Purple Dye

To prepare a purple dye for vellum or white water color paper, you must combine four ounces of Brazil Wood chips with forty ounces of water and one quarter teaspoon of alum, in a pot, and allow this mixture to simmer for three hours. You will be left with a deep burgundy-colored liquid which you should pour into a jar and allow to cool at room temperature. Once it is cool, the liquid should be stored in a refrigerator.

Dyeing the Vellum or Paper

To dye vellum or water color paper in preparation for gilding on it, you must begin by placing the vellum or paper in a shallow pan and pouring the dye into the pan with it. The vellum will curl when it becomes wet, so you will want to use flat river rocks to weigh the corners down, and keep them flat. Allow the material to sit submerged in the dye for eight hours. Then flip the material over, by which time the rocks are no longer necessary, and allow it to sit submerged for another eight hours.

To dry the material, transfer it to a sheet of glass, flatten it out, and allow it to air dry. When one side is dry, flip it over and allow the other side to dry in the same way. If buckling occurs, flatten the material out with a board.

Conclusion

"Gold speaks loudly in all medieval arts, and its words vary from the complex speeches that Duccio and Botticelli give it to the simple Magnificat! That it sings in every least provincial work. There was a time, and not so long ago, when men spoke not of the Middle Ages but of the Dark Ages. We have learned that their apparent darkness is the darkness of our own understanding. When we contemplate the history of medieval art, and summon up remembrance of what its works were in their day, and see the part played in them by the metal gold, we may well wonder whether we should not do wisely to call them not the Middle Ages but the Golden Age" (Materials 229).

We have observed, that since its nineteenth century revival, modern gilding has, in some respects, plunged backward into a kind of dark ages of its own. We have observed that when modern gilders rejected Cennini's techniques in favor of their own, the craft of gilding degenerated into the craft of the crapshoot. The uncertainty with which contemporary experts regard their craft is evinced by their own words:
"steady success in gilding can never be attained by a fixed rule, for the work does not behave in the same way twice, even on consecutive days" (Cal. Handbook I, 114 Base).
and
"It follows that we should exercise a flexible approach to the gilding processes; we can either modify the gesso ingredients, by increasing the sugar to attract more moisture, for instance, or

alter the environment in which the work is done" (Cal. Handbook II, 192-193, Jackson).

These experts are compelled to acknowledge the uncertainty of their methods because the results these methods produce are equally uncertain. In fact, gilding is a craft of precise methods which yield consistent results. In formulating my own techniques, I have bypassed the haphazard methods of the past two centuries, and have returned to those employed by Cennini and his contemporaries in gilding's golden age. I have coupled these with my own advancements to produce techniques which, I am confident, will greatly enable your own gilding endeavors.

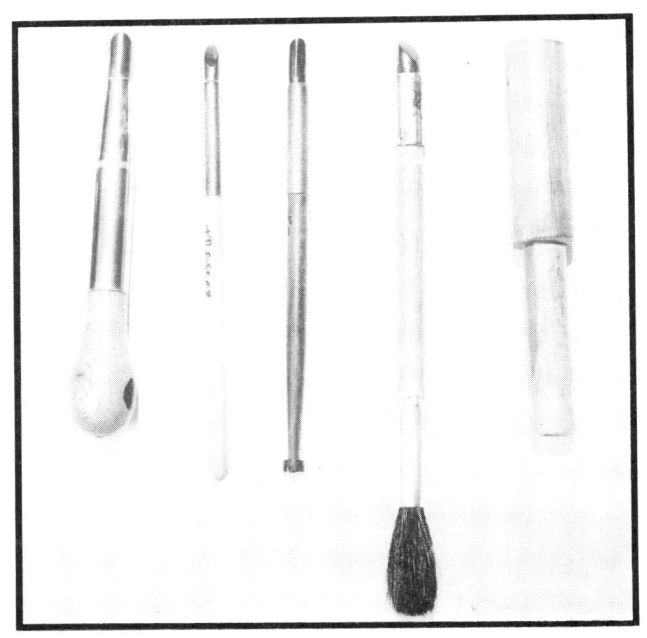

From left to right, Psilomelanite burnisher, Handmade hemitite burnishers, Breathing tube.

Glossary of Materials and Terms

Alum - a mordant used to fix color in the making of dyes.

Armenian Bole - a powder of earth, varying in color, but with salmon being the common choice among gilders because it lends a favorable tint to the gold on top of it. It does not necessarily come from Armenia. The word bole means lump.

Burnishers, Burnishing - I have discussed three different types of burnishers here: agate, psilomelanite, and true hematite. Also worth mentioning is a hound's tooth burnisher. An agate burnisher is used only for polishing because it is very smooth. It serves as a finishing tool to polish a dried gesso to a fine polish in preparation for the laying on of the gold.

While an agate burnisher is a cold burnisher, that is, it gives off no heat when used, a true hematite burnisher emits heat, enabling a user to combine it with a cold gilding surface, and thereby form a stronger bond of gold with gesso. A true hematite has a rougher surface than an agate, and not only polishes the gold, but also forges it onto the gesso base.

A true hematite is called true because synthetic alternatives are available, such as the psilomelanite burnisher. While much less costly, and while also emitting heat during burnishing, the psilomelanite is not nearly so effective as the true hematite.

To test a purported true hematite for authenticity, dampen a piece of sandpaper, and rub the burnisher over the damp area. Because of the sulphur in it, a true hematite will turn the paper a rust red. This is how hematite acquired the name of bloodstone. On the other hand, a synthetic psilomelanite burnisher will turn the paper black.

Finally, hound's tooth burnishers are both hot and cold burnishers, but again, are not nearly as effective as the true hematite.

Gesso - an Italian word meaning gypsum or Plaster of Paris. These two terms themselves are synonymous, and are common terms for gesso. The chemical term for gesso is Calcium Sulfate.

Gesso, however, is a broad and varied term. It can refer to any powder used to provide bulk to a water mixture. It can be used almost synonymously with the word paint, that is, a particularly liquid pigment. And it can be used to describe the substance acquired from mixing together, in a particular order and combination, the materials discussed above the chapter on preparing a gesso. It is this substance, forming the pedestal upon which the gold is laid, which I am referring to most often in the course of the book.

The term *gesso grosso* and *gesso sottile* are Italian terms meaning thick gesso and thin gesso, respectively. They describe two very different kinds of gesso. The former is unslaked, or coarse, thus the term gesso grosso - thick, fat - while the later is slaked, or smooth, and thus the term sottile- thin, slender, subtle. Slaked gesso is, literally, gypsum which has been mixed so vigorously that it prevents the unslaked plaster from setting, forming once again the crystalline structure in which it is found in quarries.

Glair - is the term used to describe egg white deprived of it natural stringiness by being whipped to a froth, allowed to stand, and then mixed with water. It is an external as opposed to the internal size found in a properly made gesso. In raised gilding, it is sometimes used when only a very small surface is to be gilded, and there is the need to reconstitute the gesso with this instead of water in order to provide the gesso with an added adhesive. Glair is made by beating an egg white to stiff consistency, allowing it to sit overnight.

Size - refers to the binder acquired from the careful boiling of the skins or bones of animal or fish. Size is a far more tenacious binder than blue. The term parchment size, frequently found in writings on gilding, refers to the size obtained from boiling the clippings of hide remaining after the principal portion was cut up to make parchment or vellum.

The terms glue and size, though literally quite different, are frequently used synonymously.

Gold - Gold comes in various thicknesses, purities, and forms. Standard weight gold is a term which refers to single weight gold of twenty-two karats of purity. Single weight is the thinnest form of leaf gold available, and may be compared to double and triple weight gold, though these terms, while describing thicker forms of the leaf, do not necessarily denote gold of double or triple the thickness. A karat is a measure of the purity of gold, with twenty-four karats being one hundred percent pure.

Gold of less than twenty-four karats is mixed with various alloys, giving it a necessary hardness for burnishing.

Both the patent and transfer golds used in raised gilding come in small booklets of twenty-five leaves to the book, each leaf being 3.25 inches square.

White lead - is a poisonous substance whose chemical name is lead carbonate. It is used as a filler between the needles of Plaster of Paris when making a gesso. In addition to acting as a filler for the gesso, its density and opacity lend to gesso, or to any paint for that matter, an ability to cover surfaces thoroughly in one coat.
Though it may be blackened by sulphur gases in the open air, this is not a problem when using it to gild because the gold protects it from exposure.

Although the author has not been able to come up with a substitute for white lead, the reader should be aware that *lead carbonate is extremely poisonous, and should be handled with extreme care.*

A materials list of gilding supplies is available through:

Scribes Art Shop, Inc.
568 Jefferson Shopping Plaza
Port Jefferson Station, New York 11776
(516)331-1500
(800)545-2303
Fax:(516)331-8232

Works Cited:

Base, Irene. "Gilding." The Calligrapher's Handbook. Ed. C.M. Lamb. New York: Pentalic, 1978.

De Arte Illuminandi. Daniel V. Thompson, Jr., trans. New Haven: Yale University, 1933.

Herringham, Christiana, J. The Book of the Art of Cennino Cennini. London: George Allen and Unwin, Ltd., 1899.

Hewitt, Graily. Lettering. London: Seeley Service, 1976.

Jackson, Donald. "Gilding." The Calligrapher's Handbook II. New York: Taplinger, 1986.

Johnson, Edward. Writing, Illuminating and Lettering. London: Pitman, 1977.

Mactaggart, Peter and Ann. Practical Gilding. Welwyn: Mac & Me., Ltd., 1985.

Shaw, Henry. A Handbook of the Art of Illumination. London: Bell and Daldy, 1876.

Thompson, Daniel V., trans. The Craftsman's Handbook. New York: Dover, 1960.

Thompson, Daniel V., ed. Il Libro Dell'Arte. New Haven: Yale University, 1932.

Thompson, Daniel V., The Materials and Techniques of Medieval Painting. New York: Dover, 1956.

Werner, Paul. "Dragon's Blood and Ashes." Calligraphy Idea Exchange. Philadelphia, 1984.

Footnotes to Preface:

1. Quoted in Fairfield Porter. Art In Its Own Terms. Selected Criticism 1935-1975. Edited by Rackstraw Downes. New York; Taplinger, 1979, 26.

2. Pliney. Natural History. Loeb Classical Library. Cambridge, Mass.: Harvard University Press, 1948, vol. IX, 51, 287. (Books XXXIII, 64 and XXXV, 35).

3. Theophilus Presbyter, also called Rugerus. On Divers Arts: The Treatise of Theophilus. Translated from the medieval Latin with introduction and notes by John G. Hawthorne and Cyril Stanley Smith. Chicago: University of Chicago Press, 1963; New York: Dover Publications, 1979; Chapter 23, 29-31; Chapter 29, 36-7; the transition from Pliny's recipe to one for gilding in books is problematic.

4. Daniel Varney Thompson. The Craftsman's Handbook. The Italian "Il Libro dell'Arte." Translated by Daniel Varney Thompson, Jr., New Haven and London: Yale University Press, 1933; Dover Publications, 1954. An Italian edition.

5. Paul Werner. "Dragon's Blood and Ashes; Gold Standards." Calligraphy Idea Exchange Vol. II, no. 2, 1984; 20-22.

6. Notably: Cennino Cennini. A Treatise on Painting Written by Cennino Cennini in the Year 1437; and first published in Italian in 1821, with an introduction and notes, by Signor Tambroni. Translated by Mrs. Merrifield. With an introductory preface, copious notes. London, E. Lumley, 1844; Mary Philadelphia Merrifield. Original Treatises on the Arts of Painting. 2 Vols. London, 1849; New York: Dover Publications, 1967; Theophilus was published in 1847 in a translation by Robert Hendrie; however, the first publication in England goes as far back as 1781.

7. Alice Chandler. A Dream of Order: The Medieval Ideal in XIXth Century English Literature. Lincoln: University of Nebraska Press, 1970, especially 222; On the influence of Italian rotunda gothic on Morris, cf. Peter Stansky. Redesigning the World. William Morris, the 1880's and the Arts and Crafts. Princeton, N.J.: Princeton University Press, 1985, 227; see also Joseph Dunlap. "William Morris, Calligrapher." William Morris and the Art of the Book. London: Oxford University Press, and New York: Pierpont Morgan Library, 1976, 48-170; May Morris, "Introduction," The Collected Works of William Morris, New York: Russell and Russell, 1966, Vol. 9, xvii-xxxi, gives an enchanting picture of William Morris as an illuminator.

8. A very large number of manuscripts written out by Hewitt were gilded by women - often women like Kingsford, who was married to Morris' assistance Sydney Cockerell, and was far better known as a gilder than Hewitt himself; see Anthea Callen. Women Artists of the Arts and Crafts Movement 1870-1914. New York: Pantheon Books, 1979, 186; Gillian Naylor, The Encyclopedia of Arts and Crafts: 1850-1920. New York: Dutton, 1989, 12.

PHOTO 1

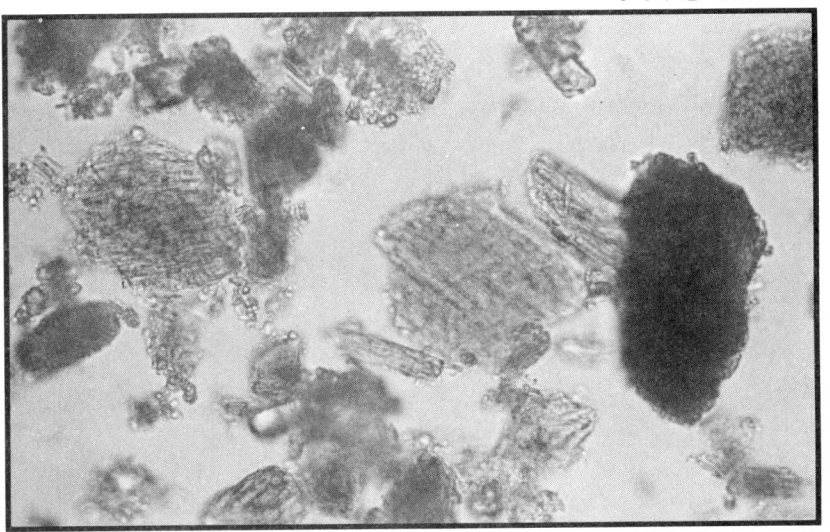

PHOTO 2

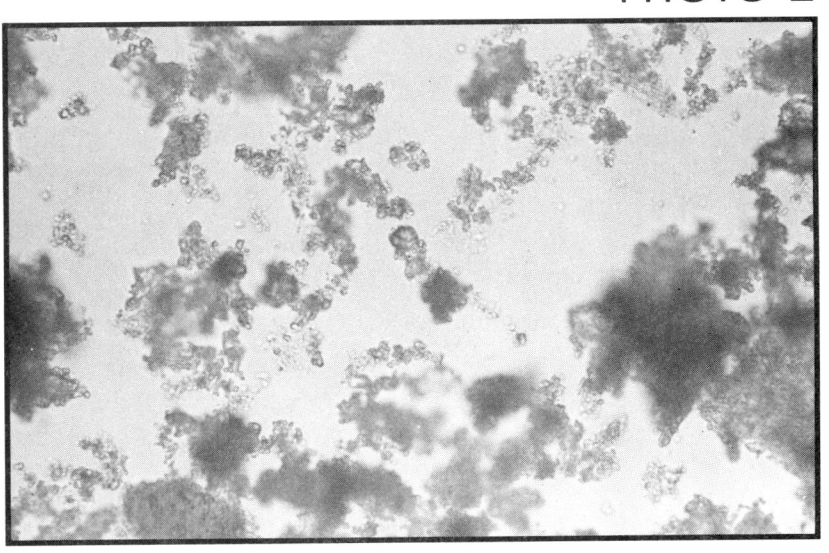

Photo 1 & 2 show the amorphous shape of unslaked Plaster of Paris (400x)

PHOTO 3

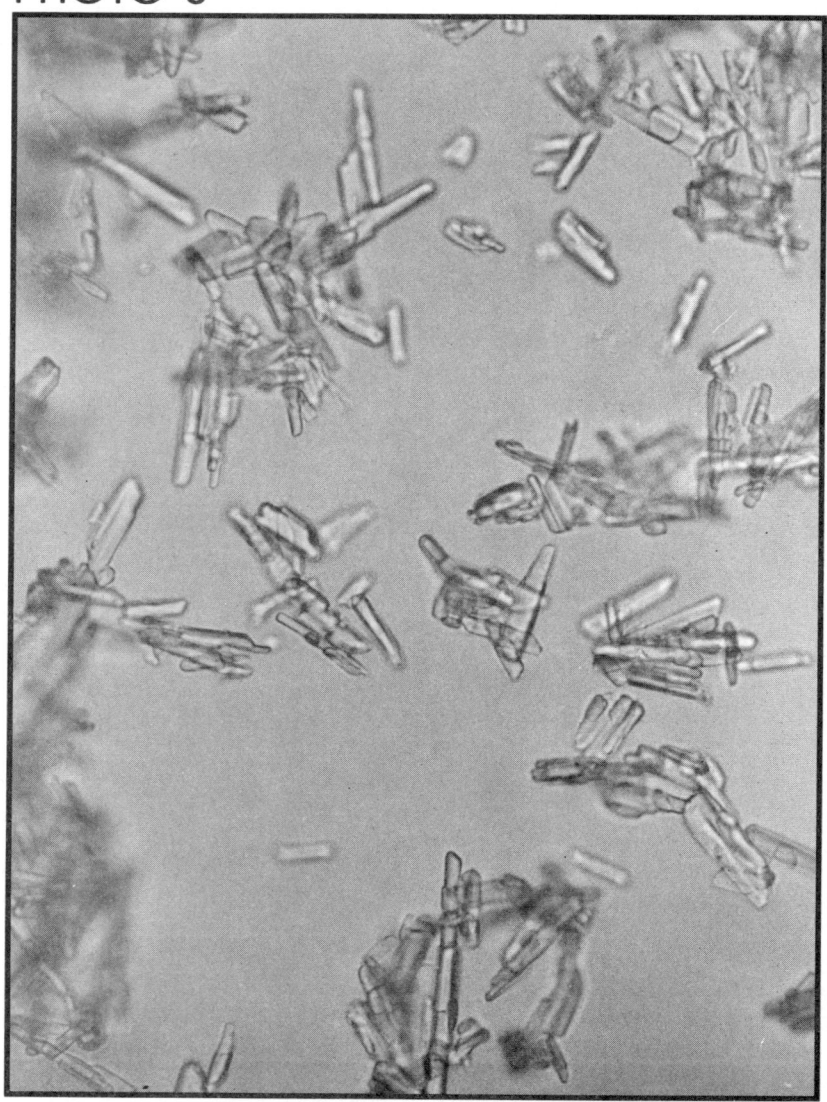

Photo 3 and 4 show slaked Plaster of Paris (by the author) notice the needle shaped properties. It is for this reason why grinding should not be done when preparing the gesso.

PHOTO 4

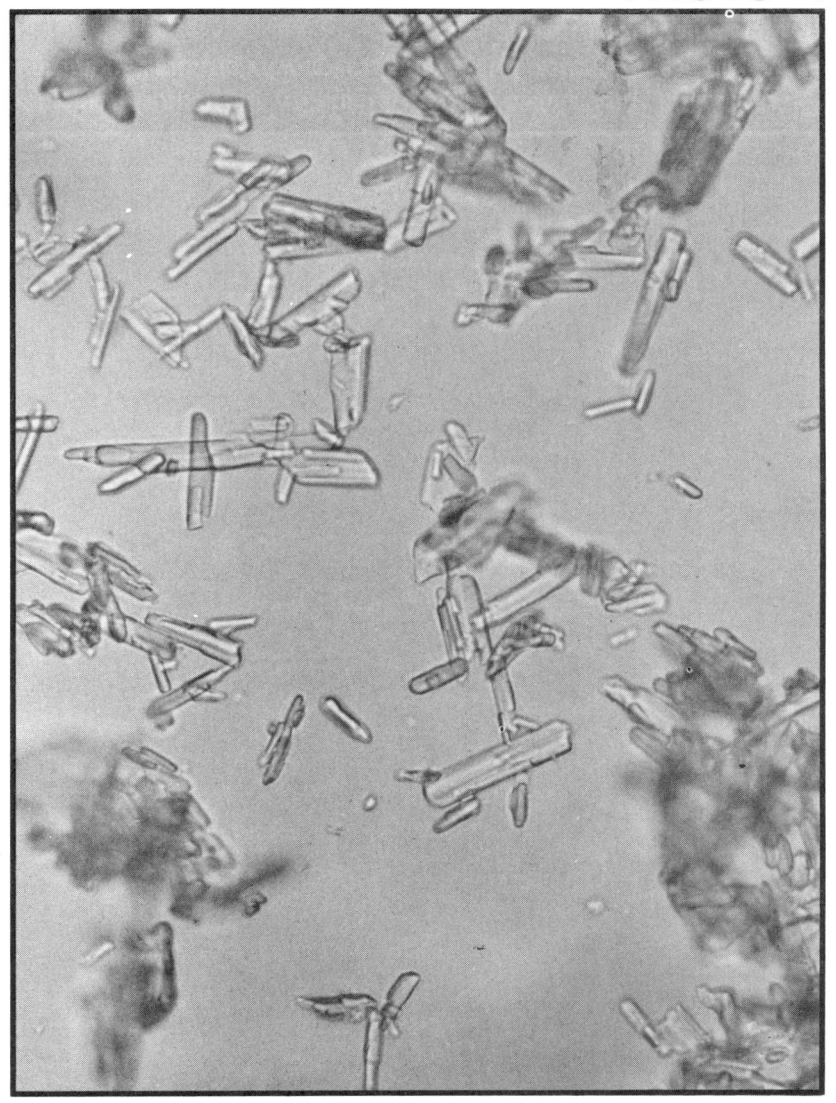

The least amount of disturbance to the structure, the more intact it remains. (400x)

PHOTO 5

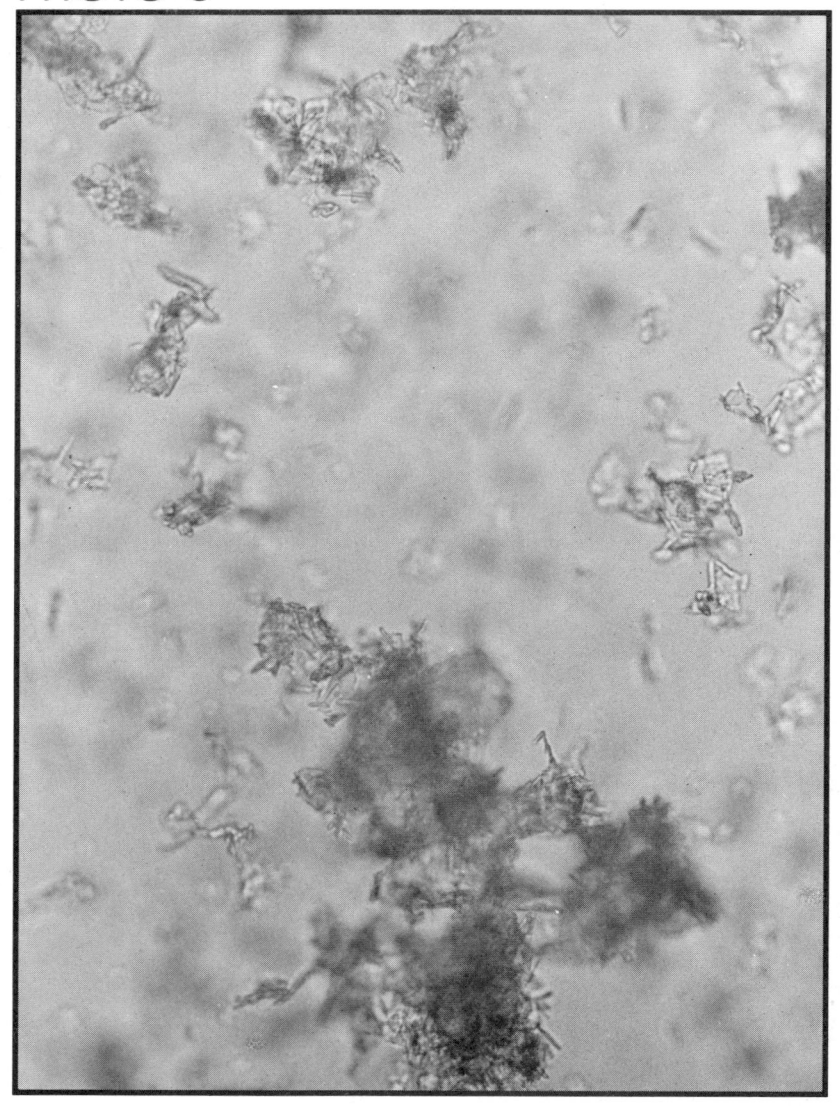

Photo 5 & 6 are but a sample of the photos showing an incomplete slaking process. Twenty samples of salked plaster most of which were purchased in the USA and England were tested and examined. Almost all plasters showed an incomplete slaking.

PHOTO 6

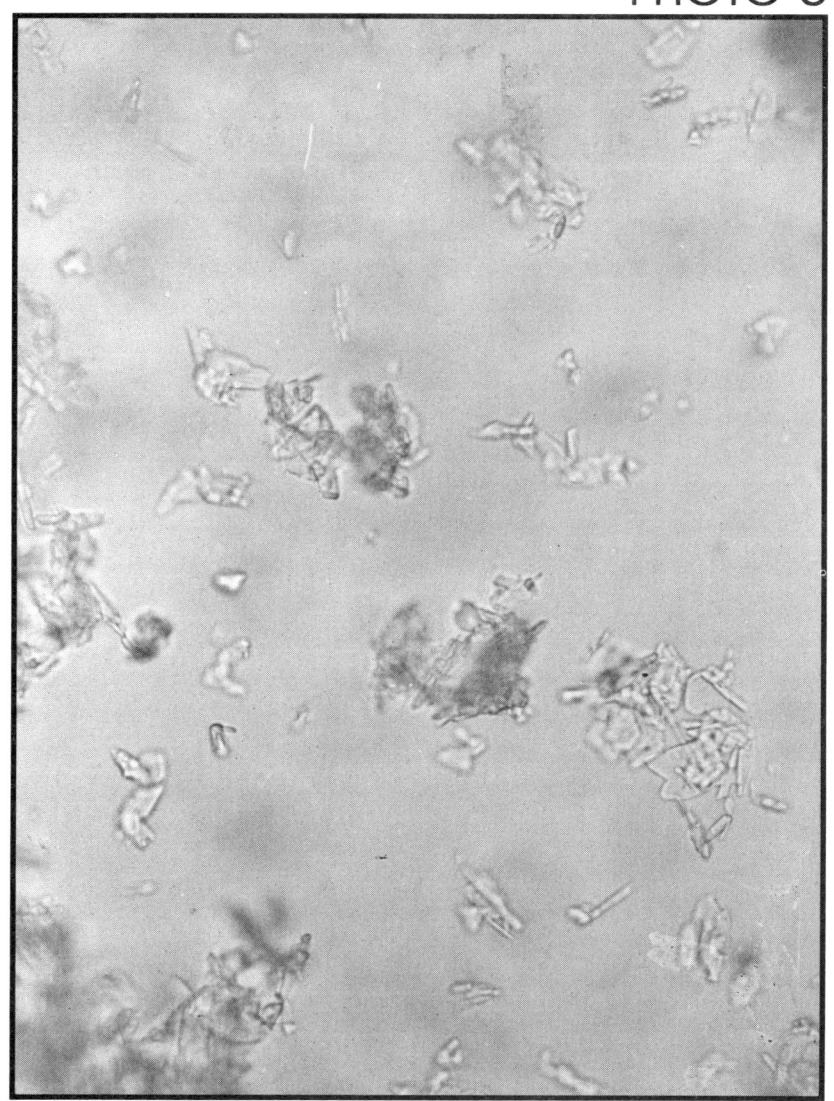

This would have a substantial effect on the gesso structure which will lead to the cracking, concavities down the center of the gesso and a complete breakup of the foundations.
Very oncosistent slaking (400x).

PHOTO 7

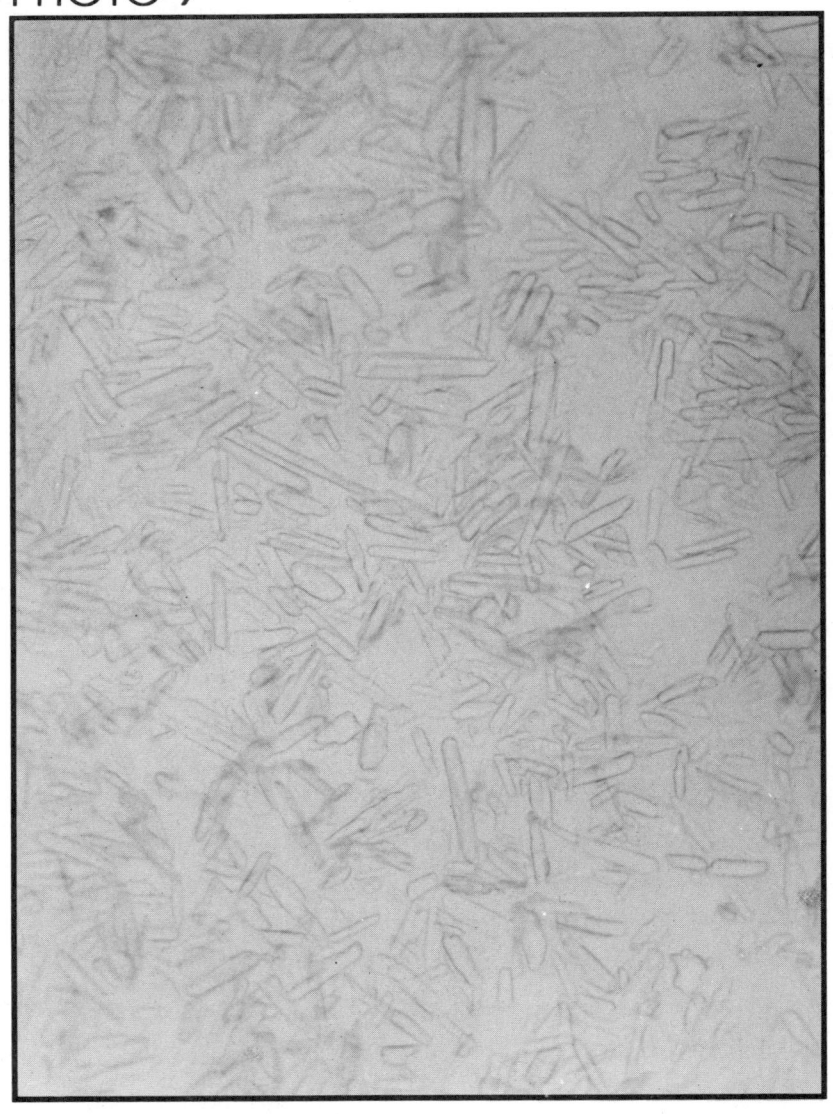

Photo 7 & 8 show the slaked plaster (used by the author) and hide glue mixed together as part 1 of the gesso process.

PHOTO 8

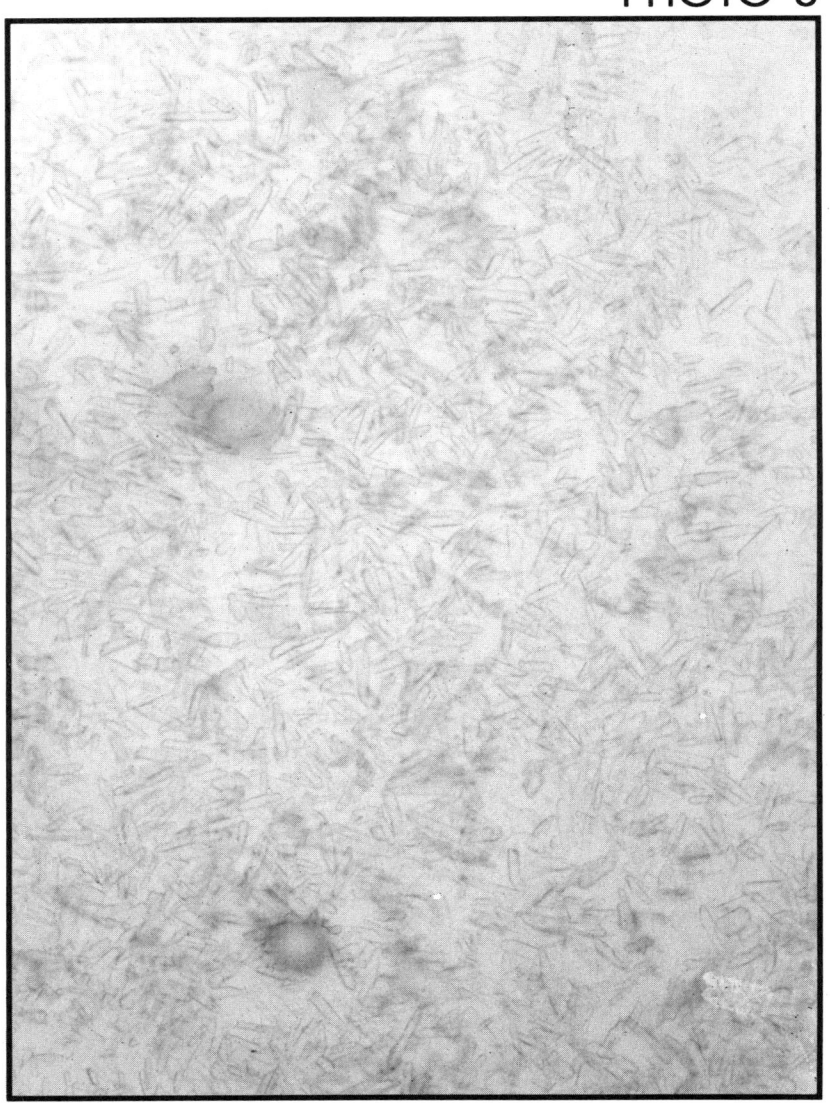

Hide glue being very soluble in water is evenly distributed and bonds the needle-like structures to each other (400x).

PHOTO 9

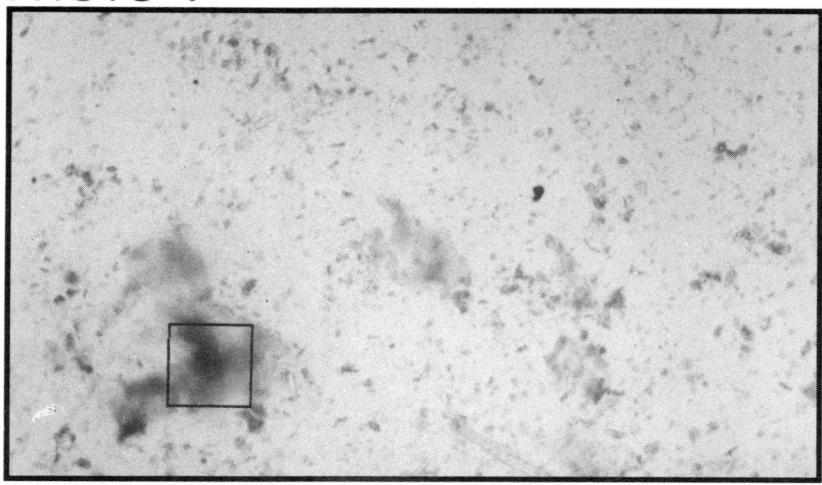

PHOTO 10

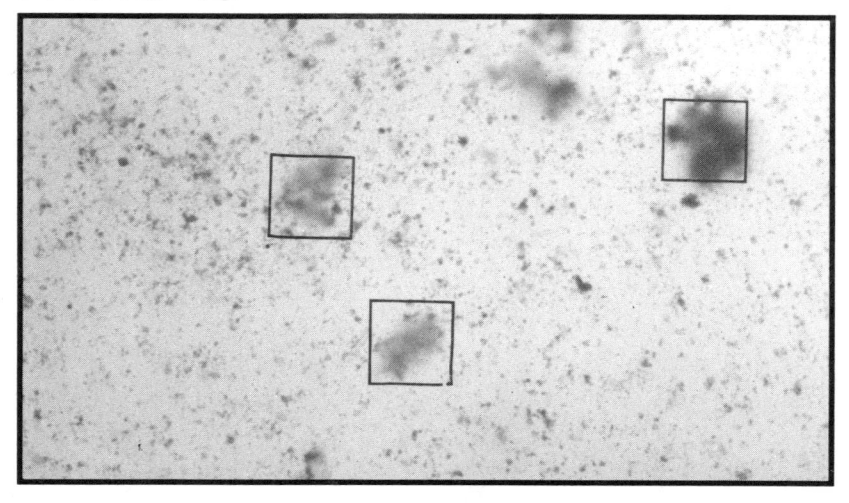

Photo 9 & 10 show the conventional gesso and dyed secotine fish glue coagulating to the various portions of the pie and buttons. Unevenly distributed glue and a very poor plaster structure has led to many a failure in gilding. The bonding breaks up twice. Once in its initial preperation and secondly in its reconstitution.

ADDENDUM TO PAGE 27

The author has been unable to find any record or evidence of Fish Glue being used in the preparation of gessos until the early 20th century. Although Hewitt introduced it into his preparation, it was well established by the 17th century as an unreliable binder and as Sir Antonio Van Dyke the great Flemish painter pointed out " It is good for nothing." -The Book Of The Art Of Cennini, Herringham translation, Pg236 see notes.

ADDENDUM TO PAGE 48

The author inadvertently neglected to mention that when slaking plaster using the PH testing method, after the plaster has settled and a reading taken, the water must be poured off and fresh distilled water added. Re-agitate the water again, allow the plaster to settle and take another reading. This should be done several times until the plaster is slaked.